What It Means to Be a Christian

Written by
Jesse Campbell

100 Devotions for Boys

978-1-4336-8568-2

Published by B&H Publishing Group
Nashville, Tennessee

Dewey Decimal Classification: 242.62
Subject Heading: SALVATION \
DEVOTIONAL LITERATURE \ BOYS

All Scripture quotations are taken from
the Holman Christian Standard Bible®, Copyright ©
1999, 2000, 2002, 2003, 2009 by Holman Bible Publishers.

2 3 4 5 6 7 8 • 19 18 17 16 15

Contents

Introduction

God is calling you into the big waves. That's why you're holding this book. It's time to leave the shore and paddle out into the deep. It's time to put your faith fully in Jesus and meet Him on the water. This is what it means to be a Christian. I'm Jesse Campbell, and I can't wait to introduce you to Jesus on a whole new level.

After a week or so of jumping around the Bible to cover some important bases about what it means to be a Christian, we will go back and forth between two tracks. Make two long, 4-inch-wide bookmarks for yourself, and make sure that you can write in pen on them. They will be like miniature journals for our journey. One bookmark will track our progress through Matthew and the other bookmark will track our super-fast tour of the Bible from Genesis through Revelation. Your Matthew bookmark should be a little longer than your "fast-track" bookmark. I promise, these bookmarks will be worth your while. We're going to do really cool things with them!

Step into the Deep

—MATTHEW 14:25–33

Step out into the deep, young man. Take a step of faith out onto the water and meet Jesus where He may be found. Before we start our routine devotionals, we're going to spend a week on the basics. *Read today's text.*

Yep, Peter just surfed without a board. Jesus was the first surfer in documented history, and Peter's sinking episode here, when he takes his eyes off of Jesus, is the first recorded wipeout.

The wind may be blowing in your life right now. You may have been through some storms that have shaken your faith like Peter's was shaken. My words to you are just an echo of Jesus' words to His disciples: "Have courage!" This journey of faith in stepping out of your comfort zone and stepping onto the water will require courage. It will take you to places you never imagined. My hope is you would make the same proclamation of Jesus that the people in the boat made in verse 33—that Jesus truly is the Son of God.

What can you do this week to step into the deep?

_____

_____

_____

_____

_____

_____

_____

_____

_____

_____

_____

_____

_____

_____

Take Up Your Cross

—MATTHEW 16:24

Read today's text. Boom. Jesus just told us what it takes to be a Christian: we must deny ourselves. To say that Jesus is Lord is to say we are choosing to no longer be lord of our own lives. Furthermore, He tells us to take up our cross.

That is such a huge statement! Jesus knows that He is going to be crucified on a cross to pay for the sins of those who believe in Him. He knows that He will take up a cross, and He does not ask us to do something that He hasn't done for us. A cross is not exactly a recliner. It's the opposite of comfortable. Jesus is telling us, as He also does in Luke 14:33, that being His disciple will cost us everything. Some people stand on the shore looking out at the waves of Christianity and are only prepared to put one foot in the water, but you can't surf with one foot on the shore. Ask yourself this question and don't get up until you're ready to answer it honestly: Are you willing to surrender everything you have to Christ?

What will you surrender?

_____

_____

_____

_____

_____

_____

_____

_____

_____

_____

_____

_____

_____

_____

_____

Confess with Your Mouth

—ROMANS 10:9

Today, we focus on repentance. *Read today's text.*

A Christian is someone who is saved, and this is one of the Bible's most clear-cut verses that straight up tells us how to be saved. First, confess that Jesus is Lord. Because Jesus rose again from the grave, we know that He is Lord. Because Jesus is my Lord, I strive to stay repentant and keep sin out of my life. Next, when you have faith, when you believe with all of your guts that Jesus died to pay the price for your sins and then rose again from the grave in victory, you are saved. That's the second half of this powerful verse.

People are not saved by repenting from sin. They repent from sin because they are saved. Somewhere out there, a person who denies Christ has decided to stop lying, but that act of repentance will not save him. There is a difference between deciding to do the right thing and repenting from sin because Jesus is Lord. All day today, think hard about the difference.

What's the difference to you?

_____

_____

_____

_____

_____

_____

_____

_____

_____

_____

_____

_____

_____

Does God Even Exist?

—HEBREWS 11:3

Do you believe that God exists? Today's text Hebrews 11:3 states, "By faith we understand that the universe was created by God's command, so that what is seen has been made from things that are not visible." *Atheism* (pronounced "ay-thee-izm") is the belief that there's no God or gods at all. The biggest flaw in this worldview is that it has no "step one" and never will. Common sense tells you nothing can come from nothingness, yet we exist. So a nonphysical Creator must have made us. Only those who believe in a Creator or creators have a step one to their beliefs.

It's by faith we believe the Creator was our God. This means we believe what the Bible says, that its claims can be investigated, and that we can see how it transforms lives every day. If you're struggling with belief in God, I want you to stay right where you are and not get up until you see the importance of the fact that nothing comes from nothing, yet we exist and the only possible explanation for our existence is a nonphysical Creator.

How have you seen God recently?

_____

_____

_____

_____

_____

_____

_____

_____

_____

_____

_____

_____

God Does Exist!

—PSALM 14:1

Today's text is Psalm 14:1 (as well as Psalm 53:1) and it says, "The fool says in his heart, 'God does not exist.'" Consider the risk of not believing in God. The French philosopher Blaise Pascal (such a stinkin' cool name) laid out the risks of atheism next to the risks of belief in God. Because God exists, the Christian risks nothing after death while the atheist risks eternity apart from God after his death. If God did not exist, the Christian would still risk nothing, but gain the benefits of the Christian life (though many Christians suffer tremendously for their faith) while the atheist gains nothing. To decide for life that God does not exist is to bet your eternal future on something that you can never know for sure and cannot re-decide after death. It is, as Psalm 14:1 says, foolish.

Today, if you are not part of a church already, you're going to need to find someone who faithfully attends a nearby, rock-solid, Bible-teaching church and commit to visit it. You may have professed disbelief in God, but it's plain to see that is foolish and not worth the risk.

What steps will you take today in your faith?

_____

_____

_____

_____

_____

_____

_____

_____

_____

_____

_____

_____

_____

_____

Repent and Be Baptized

—ACTS 2:37–38

The day that the Holy Spirit of God came in power to a huge group of believers was an awesome day. The whole thing was witnessed by a crowd of thousands who didn't believe—yet. The crowd thought the believers were drunk at nine in the morning! In response, Peter speaks up and lays out this in-your-face sermon about Jesus. Today's text is the final point of that sermon—the sermon that led about 3,000 people to Christ! *Read today's text.*

After hearing this message that confronted their sin, these people were deeply convicted. Peter tells them first to repent (Jesus is Lord, remember?) and then to be baptized. I pray that you, like these guys, would come under that same conviction. It's a beautiful kind of brokenness that leaves us bewildered in the face of the gospel. Having been shown the terrible truth of our sin and having been drawn by the Father (John 6:44) to be saved, we are left asking, "What do I do now?" Peter answers with God-breathed directness: Repent, be baptized, and receive the gift of the Holy Spirit!

Whom can you talk to today about where you are in your faith?

_____

_____

_____

_____

_____

_____

_____

_____

_____

_____

_____

_____

Be a Daydreamer

—ROMANS 8:1–11

In Acts 1:8, the resurrected Jesus (do you believe in Him?) told His remaining disciples they would receive power when the Holy Spirit came upon them. This is the Holy Spirit Peter told the crowd about in yesterday's devotional. Like Jesus, the Holy Spirit is fully God. He is the way God's presence can be known on the earth today. He transforms our lives, convicting us of sin and drawing us to do God's will. He is awesome. *Read today's text.*

To be a Christian is to be filled with the Holy Spirit. To lack the Holy Spirit, according to today's text, is to not be a Christian (verse 9). The Holy Spirit leads us away from our flesh's desire to sin (verse 4). Now, knowing the Holy Spirit is not just an emotional thing, and it's not something a Christian feels all the time. It is about transformation in our lives. Today, I want you to be a daydreamer. I want you to envision your life transformed by the Holy Spirit of God and filled with His power. I bet that even your wildest visions will still fall short of what the Holy Spirit will do in your life.

How will your life be transformed?

_____

_____

_____

_____

_____

_____

_____

_____

_____

_____

_____

_____

_____

_____

The Next Steps

—JOHN 4:23–24

Reading the Bible, praying, committing to a church, giving, and worshipping are all big parts of being a Christian. Worship is the act of telling God how great He is with our hearts, lives, words, and songs. Christians come together at our churches to worship God together. Today, Jesus teaches us about worship. *Read today's text*.

So, because God is spirit (verse 24), worshipping God is a spiritual act. Because God is so righteous, it also has to be completely "for real." That's what it means to say that true worshippers worship God in *spirit* and in *truth*. The Holy Spirit often moves powerfully in people's hearts as they worship. For some people, especially young people, that can be an intensely emotional thing that leads them to raise their hands or even cry. Worshipping in spirit and experiencing the Holy Spirit do not *have* to be emotional experiences, but they can be. What matters more is being authentic in worship. These are the kind of worshippers that God wants (verse 23). Are you up for it?

What is worship?

_____

_____

_____

_____

_____

_____

_____

_____

_____

_____

_____

_____

_____

_____

A Reminder

—JOSHUA 10:12–14

Give yourself some sort of constant reminder today on your hand. It could be with a marker, a rubber band, a string, or an angry piranha with its teeth sunk deeply into your flesh all day—whatever is going to remind you to pray. *Read today's text.*

It is truly amazing that the One who created supernovae, whirlpool galaxies, and black holes in space would listen to man at all. Now, does God listen to the prayers of those who live in sin against Him? James 5:16 teaches that the prayer of a righteous man is powerful and effective. Are you righteous? Isaiah 59:2 teaches that our sins block us from God so that He does not listen. Have you confessed sin to God to be forgiven (1 John 1:9)? John 9:31 teaches that God listens to our prayers when we do His will. Have you done God's will? As you are reminded to pray today, think on this: why should God listen to our prayers? Psalm 145:17–20 will help you. May you become a righteous man like Joshua, who prayed massive prayers according to God's will, a man who saw the sun stand still.

What has God reminded you of?

_____

_____

_____

_____

_____

_____

_____

_____

_____

_____

_____

_____

_____

He Has a Plan

—MATTHEW 1:16–19

We have jumped all around the Bible, but today we are about to get into a groove. Speaking of grooves, the two bookmarks we talked about in the introduction—one for the Gospel of Matthew and the other for our quick tour through the Bible from Genesis. Today, we start the book of Matthew; the first of the four Gospels. It begins with this huge list of names, but I just want you to skim through that before really reading verses 16–19. *Read today's text.*

Did you catch my name "Jesse" in the list? Ha! My son Asa's name is there too. Now, look at how rough things were before Jesus' birth. Jesus was born into a story of exile, scandal, and divorce. Yet, God knew exactly what He was doing. The forty-two generations listed here do not complete the genealogy. God knew what He was doing for several centuries even before He created the world. If life is really rough right now, remember that God sees how it all ends and He has a plan. He gave us Jesus in the midst of a dark time, and He can give you deliverance in the midst of your dark times.

List who you can go to in tough times.

_____
_____
_____
_____
_____
_____
_____
_____
_____
_____
_____
_____
_____
_____
_____

A Christian

—MATTHEW 1:20–25

Did you know that the word *Christian* was actually origi-nally a put-down? It was first used in the city of Antioch to describe believers in Jesus (Acts 11:26). The word *Christian* means "little Christ" and the word *Christ* is not actually Jesus' last name as some people think. It is a title, and only Jesus is worthy of it. When the believers in Jesus were called "little Christs" or "Christians," they actually liked it and it stuck. So, what does it mean to be a Christian? It means to embrace a two-thousand-year-old insult! *Read today's text.*

As a young man, you need to consider the example of Joseph. He had reason to believe that Mary had been unfaithful to him, but instead of making a big deal of it, he intended to break things off quietly. Then, when the angel spoke to him, he obeyed even though what the angel described was physically impossible. That is a man of faith, and that is the kind of man I want you to be. He believed that Jesus would be the Christ. He believed that Jesus would save us from our sins and so he obeyed in faith.

What kind of man do you want to be?

_____

_____

_____

_____

_____

_____

_____

_____

_____

_____

_____

_____

_____

Faking It

—MATTHEW 2:1–8

Read today's text. Look at what a fake McFakerson Herod is. He pretends to be someone who worshipped Jesus, but he actually just wanted to have Jesus killed. Herod was threatened by the prophecies that said Jesus would lead the Israelites. So, Herod said the things that a Christian would say (verse 8).

Fake Christians say the right things and claim to worship Jesus just like Herod, but the truth is that they are hostile toward Christianity. I mean, Herod even told the wise men to search "carefully" as though he cared about Jesus! Can you believe this guy? Now, if you were to encounter Herod and hear him claim to be a Christian, you would probably see right through him. The wise men did. That's why they didn't report back to him. If Herod were the only "Christian" you met, you might, like many people, think, *Wow, all Christians are hypocrites!* You would be wrong. What does it mean to be a Christian? It means more than just saying the right words like Herod. It means truly believing in Jesus like the wise men.

How do you fake it in life?

_____

_____

_____

_____

_____

_____

_____

_____

_____

_____

_____

_____

God's Heart

—GENESIS 1:1–27

Don't forget to use two editable bookmarks to make finding your daily passage in the Bible easier. Keep one in Matthew and the other on our fast track tour of the Bible from Genesis through Revelation. Today, we read the first verses of the Bible. *Read today's text.*

What you have just read is the only comprehensive and sensible (meaning it covers all of its bases and makes sense) story of how the whole universe came into existence out of nothingness. It also answers questions that science cannot explain. Questions like, "Where did the universe come from?" and "Where did the design and order we see come from?" No other atheistic (meaning written or spoken by someone who does not believe in any religion) or religious account comes close. Did you notice how, after every stage of creation, God looked with great affection at what He just made? Today, think on what that shows about God's heart toward you. You are a part of God's beloved creation.

How does creation show you God's love?

_____

_____

_____

_____

_____

_____

_____

_____

_____

_____

_____

_____

Covenants

—GENESIS 2:15–16; 3:1–7

When God created the earth, every physical thing was perfect. Evil existed, but only in spiritual beings like Satan and his demons, which were fallen angels. In today's passages, we see the fall of man take place. We see God's perfect creation robbed of its perfection by sin. *Read today's texts.*

If it were impossible for man to disobey God, then it could not truly be said that man obeyed God. So, God placed this tree in the garden, and the only command Adam and Eve were given was not to eat of it. That tree and God's command made Adam and Eve free—free to obey or disobey God. When Satan appeared as a snake and completely twisted God's words to tempt Eve, Adam and Eve disobeyed God. This was the first sin and is sometimes called "the original sin." Things changed not only for Adam and Eve, but also for all of mankind to come and even the world that God created. God's beloved creation was now separated from Him by sin, so God made the first of a series of covenants to redeem mankind.

What changed for all of us after the original sin?

The Magi

—MATTHEW 2:9–12

Today, we get back in touch with the wise men, also called "Magi." They were paying close attention to the prophecies of the Old Testament and saw the star that they knew would lead them to Jesus. The prophecies these Magi studied were four hundred years old! Between the end of the last book of the Old Testament and the beginning of the New Testament, God did not reveal any more words to be written down in the Bible for four hundred years. That means that the people who first received those Old Testament promises from God did not see them come to pass. Neither did their children, grandchildren, or great grandchildren. Yet, in His silence, God was still working. *Read today's text.*

These Magi were overjoyed beyond measure (verse 10) because their faith in the midst of God's silence was proven worthwhile. Though God is silent, His promises are always true!

List the promises God has made for you.

_____

_____

_____

_____

_____

_____

_____

_____

_____

_____

_____

_____

_____

Herod's Freak-out

—MATTHEW 3:1–12

Now, after the Magi saw Jesus and were warned not to go back to Herod (the fake fakety McFakerson), Herod royally flips out and goes on a murderous rampage. Joseph is warned to take Jesus and Mary to Egypt for a while until Herod dies. Then, they move to the small town of Nazareth. These events fulfill Old Testament prophecies. Herod's freak-out was prophesied by Jeremiah, the move to Egypt was prophesied by Hosea, and the move to Nazareth was prophesied by multiple Old Testament prophets. *Read today's text.*

I want you to be a wild man like this locust-eating John the Baptist. He boldly proclaimed that the long-awaited Christ was soon coming to the earth and told people to be baptized as they confessed their sins. He told people to repent—to turn away from sin. If I may be a little like John the Baptist, I want to likewise tell you to get ready because Jesus Christ is coming your way. Are you ready to repent from sin and follow Him? You may not end up wearing camel hair like John the Baptist, but following Jesus will *radically* change your life!

How can you radically change your life?

_____

_____

_____

_____

_____

_____

_____

_____

_____

_____

_____

_____

_____

Spiritual Goals

—MATTHEW 3:13–17

On your bookmark that tracks our progress through Matthew, write down a spiritual goal. If you have come to believe fully in Jesus and His resurrection, if you have come closer than ever before to becoming a Christian, or if you are drifting away from Christ, indicate that now on your bookmark along with today's date. *Read today's text.*

In Mark 1:7, John the Baptist said that he was not worthy to stoop down and tie the strap of Jesus' sandals, and yet now he has the enormous honor of baptizing Jesus! Yep, Jesus Himself was baptized. Cool, huh? Baptism is this incredible cause for celebration, and it's deeply impactful to watch if you understand what it signifies and where it came from. So, what about your baptism? Just think: you journaled where you stand with Jesus today on your bookmark. That same bookmark might one day record the date of your baptism! Today, think about the idea of baptism and how amazing it is to share in something Jesus went through Himself.

Write down your spiritual goals.

_____

_____

_____

_____

_____

_____

_____

_____

_____

_____

_____

_____

_____

God's Perfect Word

—GENESIS 3:15

The Bible is God's perfect Word. According to 2 Timothy 3:16, it is inspired by God. According to John 1:1, it is Jesus in word form. Make a note of today's devotional on your bookmark because God is about to make a prophecy in the first book of the Bible that we'll see come true in the last book. *Read today's text.*

To understand this prophecy, you must understand that Jesus was born of a virgin. This means that the part of Jesus that was fully human came not from Joseph, or any other man, but from woman—Mary. On the cross, as Jesus was pierced and crushed because of our sins (Isaiah 53:5), Satan, the snake upon whom Genesis 3:15's curse was spoken, "struck Jesus' heel." If your heel has been struck, you have been wounded. If your head is crushed, however, you have been defeated, and that's the victory Jesus will have over Satan! So, all the way back to the Garden of Eden, thousands of years ago, even though it looked like sin ruined everything, God declared His ultimate victory over it—through Jesus!

What was the ultimate victory?

_____

_____

_____

_____

_____

_____

_____

_____

_____

_____

_____

_____

_____

The Wrath of God

—GENESIS 7:11–16

God is the Creator and Champion of everything that is good. He is our Hero. He conquers evil and pours out His wrath upon it. Yes, our God has wrath, and that wrath is reserved for sin and evil. In fact, He would not truly be loving if He just allowed our sin to overtake us. He would not truly be loving if He allowed us to be swept away by evil. Instead of standing idly by while His beloved creation falls, He picks a fight with evil and conquers it with His wrath. *Read today's text.*

The flood was God's wrath poured out over sin and evil, but those who loved and obeyed Him were spared. God protected Noah and his family because Noah was faithful to God even though no one else was. The wrath of God is serious business, but God's grace upon those who love Him is incredibly beautiful news. Through the rainbow, God promised never to pour out His wrath this way again (Genesis 9:13). However, God poured out His wrath on evil in other ways later in history, and the Bible has prophecies of His coming wrath that have yet to be fulfilled.

What was God's promise?

_____

_____

_____

_____

_____

_____

_____

_____

_____

_____

_____

_____

_____

Temptation

—MATTHEW 4:1–11

Jesus was tested in every way, yet He did not sin (Hebrews 4:15). It's not like Jesus has no idea what you are going through when you face the temptation to violate God's laws. He has been there! In fact, He was tempted by Satan directly. *Read today's text.*

This is one of two passages in the whole Bible that describe a conversation between God and Satan. The other one is in the book of Job, and in both cases Satan is arrogant enough to think that He knows better than God. However, Satan is proven wrong. How did Jesus conquer this temptation? He quoted verses from the Bible. Now, Jesus didn't just pull random words out without considering which words came before or after them. That is what Satan did, and it's called "quoting Scripture out of context." Instead, Jesus used the Bible like a sword (Ephesians 6:17; Hebrews 4:12), quoting the Scriptures in accordance with what they originally meant, and Satan was defeated. If Jesus did it, then we need to do it as well!

Find a Scripture you love and write it down here.

_____

_____

_____

_____

_____

_____

_____

_____

_____

_____

_____

_____

_____

Follower of Jesus

—MATTHEW 4:18-22

At this point in the history of Jesus, things began to get difficult for His followers. John the Baptist was thrown in prison (verse 12), and Jesus began to tell people to repent because the kingdom of heaven had come near (verse 17). *Read today's text.*

What does it mean to be a Christian? It means to be a follower of Jesus, forsaking everything else and just leaving it behind because Jesus is Lord. It means repenting from sin as Jesus instructs us. It means dropping our nets and following him. Peter and Andrew were professional fishermen, and they dropped their precious nets to follow Jesus. They even left their expensive boat! What is your net? What is keeping you from surrendering everything to Jesus as Lord? Right now, as I finish writing this, I want you to know that I am praying for you in the moment you finish this devotional—that God would draw heavily upon your heart to drop everything and follow Jesus as Lord, repenting from sin and surrendering your life to Him. Drop everything and follow Jesus, young man!

How can you follow Jesus?

_____

_____

_____

_____

_____

_____

_____

_____

_____

_____

_____

_____

_____

_____

_____

Jesus' Heart

—MATTHEW 4:23–25

Read today's text. Jesus healed many people while on the earth. This was not His primary objective, but it was a big part of His ministry. Sometimes, as in Matthew 9:30, Jesus healed people and then told them to keep it a secret. If Jesus were swamped with people who needed to be healed, then His ministry as the Messiah, the Christ, the One who came to save us from our sins, would have been overwhelmed. Besides, the people He healed eventually passed away anyway.

So, what should we do with these Bible stories about miracles? They were put in the Bible for a reason, right? So, what is their purpose? They tell us about Jesus' heart. They reveal to us part of the nature of God. To be a Christian is to be healed—healed of sin, the disease that condemns us to hell apart from God. Today, see people through Jesus' eyes. See yourself through Jesus' eyes as well. If you have headphones, listen to Brandon Heath's song "Give Me Your Eyes" as you walk from class to class and let it inspire you to have the eyes of the Healer.

How do you look through Jesus' eyes?

_____

_____

_____

_____

_____

_____

_____

_____

_____

_____

_____

_____

_____

Strong Faith

—GENESIS 22:1–12

My son Aiden was born without a windpipe. The surgeries it took to keep him alive were a bi-weekly trip to the darkest place a parent can go. We knew that each surgery could be the end of his life. So, we prayed over him before each surgery a prayer inspired by today's text. We said, "God, because You gave us Your Son, we give you ours." *Read today's text.*

When God asked Abraham to do something shocking and unprecedented (meaning it had never happened before), Abraham obeyed. That is strong faith. In the end, Abraham got to keep Isaac as the whole thing was just a test of his faith. It was also God's way of showing what would happen with Jesus at the crucifixion thousands of years later. Just as Abraham gave up his only son and received him back, God gave us His only Son and received Him back. This is what it means to be a Christian: it means to have faith in God's promises the way Abraham had faith in God's promises and to obey God's commands the way Abraham obeyed God's commands.

What does having faith mean to you?

Chosen by God

—GENESIS 32:24–31

In making a nation of the Jews and showing them His favor, God was laying the foundation for New Testament Christianity. We see Jesus born in the Gospels at the start of the New Testament, but we get these cool glimpses of Him in the Old Testament, too. Both God's old covenant with the Jews and these appearances of Jesus in the Old Testament show this beautiful sense of foreshadowing and prove that God had this plan to redeem mankind from sin all along from the very beginning. *Read today's text.*

Jacob and Esau were chosen by God to be the fathers of nations—Israel, which God loved, and Edom, which God hated (Romans 9:11–13). So, there you have the story of the name Israel. Isn't it funny, though, that we don't learn the name of God's wrestling representative? In verse 29, He simply doesn't answer the question. Thousands of years later, we learn a new name for God and that is "Jesus." Are you wrestling with Jesus today? Is God the Father calling on you to be saved (John 6:44)?

What are you wrestling with today?

_____

_____

_____

_____

_____

_____

_____

_____

_____

_____

_____

_____

_____

_____

A Shocking Moment

—MATTHEW 5:1–12

Back to the book of Matthew! Jesus is about to begin the greatest sermon of all time. It's called "The Sermon on the Mount" because He taught it on the side of a mountain to a large crowd. The opening of the sermon focuses on what it means to be blessed by God. The kind of blessedness Jesus is talking about goes way beyond just the good mood you're in after eating ice cream covered in bacon; it's the kind of peace that can't be taken away by a slow Internet connection. This opening is called "The Beatitudes." *Ready today's text.*

This opening was shocking to its original hearers. Those who are poor in spirit, who mourn, who are gentle, who hunger and thirst, and who are persecuted and insulted don't seem like they would be counted as blessed, but to be a Christian is to see things differently from the rest of the world's perspective. Are you prepared to be insulted for the sake of Christ? If so, you are ready to be truly blessed!

How can you see things differently?

_____

_____

_____

_____

_____

_____

_____

_____

_____

_____

_____

_____

_____

26

Unsalty Salt

—MATTHEW 5:13–16

What is the point of salt that has absolutely no flavor? What is the point in turning on a light and then covering it up completely? Salt that has no flavor is useless, and a light that's covered up doesn't serve its purpose. Likewise, a Christian who doesn't act like a Christian is useless for God's kingdom, and a Christian who tries to hide his or her Christianity is not serving his or her purpose. *Read today's text.*

Jesus tells us that we are the salt of the earth. Christians who don't obey God's laws or carry out God's mission are like a bunch of salt that isn't salty. You can't do a thing with it besides throw it out. Also, the imagery of unsalty salt being trampled on by men gives us this picture of Christians whose faith is fruitless and weak just getting trampled. Ouch. It doesn't make sense to turn on a light and then cover it up, and if you become a Christian, God sees you as a light that He is switching on. If you're a Christian, I want you to be of use to God today and shine.

How can God use you?

_____

_____

_____

_____

_____

_____

_____

_____

_____

_____

_____

_____

_____

_____

Bulldozing Pride

—MATTHEW 5:17–22

All right, today's text could be kind of a bummer. Jesus is about to enter the phase of the Sermon on the Mount in which He takes the Old Testament laws to their fullest extent and shows all of us just how drastically short we fall from God's standards. If you began today's devotional with even a little bit of pride, it's about to get bulldozed. *Read today's text.*

Whoa. You all right, dude? That text is a blow to the gut. Jesus starts by holding up the law and saying that He is the fulfillment of it (we'll talk more about that fact later) and then, right out of the gate, shows us that every one of us who has ever called someone a fool or a moron is just as guilty as a murderer before God's law, and that's just the beginning. (See also verses 27–28; Romans 7–8; and Hebrews 10.) These laws were never meant to be enough to save us, but to show us how much we need God's grace. At this point, Jesus is establishing the necessity for His upcoming crucifixion. On the cross, Jesus paid the price that wrecks like you and I could never pay.

List why you need God's grace.

You Are Being Called by Name

—EXODUS 3:1–12

Read today's text. This Moses guy is about to be the leader of God's chosen nation—the Israelites who descended from Abraham's son Isaac about whom we read in yesterday's devotional. In the Old Testament days, the Israelites and those who became a part of their nation were God's people, and God used this nation to show the rest of the world His favor and to lay the groundwork for all who believe to be saved. It was through this nation that God would bring about Jesus. At the time that this passage takes place, God's people were enslaved and hurting. God always hears us when we cry out to Him in pain.

Now, think on the way that God called on Moses by name. I believe He is calling you by name as well. I believe that is why you have made it this far into this book. Otherwise, you would have stopped reading long ago, yet here you are. God is calling. Right now, no matter how silly it seems, I want you to take your shoes off the way that Moses did and listen to that call of God on your heart.

Listen. What is God saying to you?

A Hardened Heart

—EXODUS 14:21–31

Moses answers God's call to free the Israelites from Pharaoh's rule, but Pharaoh's heart is hardened. Even in the face of terrible plagues, Pharaoh's heart is hard, and he does not listen to Moses. While Pharaoh was free to make up his own mind and reject this word from God through Moses (which he did over and over), God was in control and had decided that He would even use Pharaoh's wicked stubbornness to do something beautiful (Exodus 6:1). Also, each of these seemingly random plagues was designed to show how our God was more powerful than one of the Egyptians' false gods. For example, the Egyptian goddess Heqet had the head of a frog, but the frogs only obeyed God in the second of the 10 plagues. Now, it's time for the nation of Israel to be baptized Old Testament style (1 Corinthians 10:2–3). *Read today's text.*

How has your heart been hardened?

_____

_____

_____

_____

_____

_____

_____

_____

_____

_____

_____

_____

_____

In Secret

—MATTHEW 6:1–4

I was once given a donation for my church's global missions program. The contributor handed me a check for $30,000 and told me to keep it a secret. That person understood *today's text*.

Being a Christian does not mean showing off how righteous you are. When people put on a show about how much they do, they will get nothing more than that fleeting recognition—recognition that is often negative. However, if we are secretive about the good things that we do for people who are in need, then God will bless us way beyond a few Facebook likes (verse 4). People who do such awesome things in a secretive way are not playing games and trying to impress people. Instead, they are actually impressive. They are the real deal, and that's the kind of faith Jesus calls us to. Today, see what it's like to do something awesome for someone, something only God knows. Be generous, and let that generosity be real.

Do something awesome in secret today.

_____

_____

_____

_____

_____

_____

_____

_____

_____

_____

_____

_____

_____

What's the Deal?

—MATTHEW 6:5–15

After Jesus teaches about how far we fall from the law (5:17–22), He tells us to cut sin out of our lives (5:29–30). After teaching us the blessing of secretive giving, He applies the same truth to the concept of prayer and then shows us how it's done. *Read today's text.*

While it's a beautiful thing to pray the Model Prayer together as large groups of people that sound like a zombie support group, that's not really its purpose. Anyway, Jesus says in verse 9 that we "should pray like this" and then He lays out the prayer. So, if you're a Christian, as you pray today, start by praising God (verses 9–10), then ask God what you need for today (verse 11), ask for forgiveness and commit to God that you will forgive others (verse 12), and ask God to keep you out of the boxing ring with temptation (verse 13). If you want to end with some more praise, then absolutely do so. Though that last sentence isn't in all of our ancient copies of the Bible, it's still a good idea and God's worthy. If you're not a Christian yet, what's the deal?

Write out your prayer for today.

_____

_____

_____

_____

_____

_____

_____

_____

_____

_____

_____

_____

_____

The Global Status

—MATTHEW 7:13–14

Read today's text. Most of the people in the world are not Christians. This is a huge deal because Christ is the only way to be saved. A research firm called the Barna Group has found that more than 60 percent of the world's population identifies with either no religion at all, or with a religion other than Christianity. To be a Christian is to be outnumbered.

With permission, use Google to find "The Global Status of Evangelical Christianity" map. This map uses the research of leading global missions organizations to show where the Christians of the world can be found. The green dots indicate a presence of Christianity, the red indicate a lack of Christianity, and the gray areas are unknown. I know this is a heavy realization, but it is an important one. It is a huge part of what God used to call me to give my life to ministry—to sharing the gospel with the world—and I'm so grateful to have seen peoples' lives changed by the gospel of Christ all over the world.

What color dots would cover your school?

_____

_____

_____

_____

_____

_____

_____

_____

_____

_____

_____

_____

_____

_____

God's Commandments

—EXODUS 20:1–17

At this point, God has just divinely swept the Israelites out of slavery, brought them through the Red Sea in a sort of Old Testament baptism (1 Corinthians 10:1–2), and is going to write down teachings for them with His own hand. Now, while God is always faithful, Israel goes back and forth in their faithfulness to God. They would obey some of the time (the book of Joshua), and then they would live in outright sin and rebellion at other times (the book of Judges). Now, we're not going to beat up on Israel for their sin. We have our own. Let's *read today's Scripture.*

While the laws under God's Old Testament covenant(s) regarding how Israel was supposed to worship back then are no longer binding over us, the Old Testament laws that taught right from wrong are still binding because God's character has not changed. To be a Christian is to obey God's commands (John 14:15), and these commandments are clear. So, compare your life now to where these commands teach that it ought to be.

What does God promise to give you?

_____

_____

_____

_____

_____

_____

_____

_____

_____

_____

_____

_____

_____

_____

Joshua, Jesus, and Yeshua

—JOSHUA 1:1–9

The book of Joshua proves that Jesus was part of the plan all along, even back in the early centuries BC (meaning "Before Christ"). The names "Joshua" and "Jesus" are both forms of the name "Yeshua." Just as Joshua led the Israelites across the Jordan River into God's promised land, Jesus leads us to the promised land. Moses, the Israelites' first leader, who gave them the old covenant laws, died on the bank of the Jordan River, leaving Joshua to lead the people into a new era just as Jesus would do for us. Joshua (Yeshua) foreshadowed Jesus (Yeshua). *Read today's text.*

The Bible is a beautiful tapestry, and this thread runs from history's ancient times to prophecy's future. Jesus has been here all along, and He is coming again! To believe this in such a way that your life is permanently impacted is to be a Christian. Become a Christian by the Holy Spirit's pull and your heart's faith-filled belief in Jesus. The Christian can be strong and courageous because the Lord is with him wherever he goes.

How is the Lord with You?

_____

_____

_____

_____

_____

_____

_____

_____

_____

_____

_____

_____

_____

An Overflowing Tree

—MATTHEW 7:15–29

Read Matthew 7:15–20. When you see oranges growing on a tree, chances are extremely high that you're looking at an orange tree. In a similar way, you can look at the "fruit" of someone's life and tell if he's a Christian. Here in Orlando, we see orange trees everywhere, and one of my students said that when he sees an orange tree overflowing with oranges, he prays that his life would be just like that—overflowing with good works and producing other Christians.

Now, we're about to read one of the toughest and scariest passages in Scripture. *Read Matthew 7:21–29.* You can't fake Christianity. You can't just say the words. People who are truly Christians will act on God's commands (verse 24). People who aren't will say the right things and even make some pretty convincing gestures (verse 22), but it's all for show as they never really knew God to begin with. Resolve now in your journey to true Christianity that you will live out your faith in raw authenticity, overflowing with Christian fruit.

What kind of fruit is showing in your life?

_____

_____

_____

_____

_____

_____

_____

_____

_____

_____

_____

_____

Mind-Blowing Miracles

—MATTHEW 8:1-17

Get ready for a powerhouse passage full of mind-blowing miracles. Jesus is on a healing rampage. *Read today's text*. As you do, notice the faith involved, the grace of God, and Jesus' willingness to heal.

In the first miracle (verses 1–4), this man knew that it was not a question of Jesus' ability to heal, but whether it was His will. In the second miracle (verses 5–13), there is incredible faith on the part of the centurion, and it is partially in response to that faith that Jesus heals this man. The man who was healed may have had no faith at all! Can you imagine what that was like for everyone at the centurion's house? Suddenly, that sick dude got up and started running around! Now, this third section is a series of miracles, and they all fulfilled Isaiah's prophecy about Jesus centuries before He came. These miracles reveal that Jesus' heart is overwhelmingly merciful. He takes our weaknesses. He carries our diseases. This is what it means to be a Christian.

What was revealed to you after reading the text for today?

_____

_____

_____

_____

_____

_____

_____

_____

_____

_____

_____

_____

_____

Big Crowds

—MATTHEW 8:18–22

Read today's text. I love big crowds. I love the electrifying energy, the deafening sound. I love raising my hands and accidently bumping into the people inches from my shoulders. When a church service or Christian event is crowded to the point that I can't hear my own voice as I belt out worship lyrics slightly off key at the top of my lungs, I go home with my heart filled to the top and my voice sore for the next two days. Jesus, however, was suspicious of big crowds.

In today's text, Jesus actively discourages a super enthusiastic potential disciple from following Him. He says, "The Son of Man [that's an Old Testament title for Jesus] has no place to lay His head," to say that He was essentially living a homeless lifestyle and anyone who comes with Him must do the same. He even treats this guy whose father had recently passed away with this really harsh and blunt challenge. In Luke 14:25–30, Jesus gives a similar teaching about those who aren't willing to take up their crosses and give what it takes to follow Jesus. Follow Jesus no matter the cost, my student!

What does today's verse say to you?

_____

_____

_____

_____

_____

_____

_____

_____

_____

_____

_____

_____

_____

_____

The Winning Team

—JOSHUA 5:13–15

To be a Christian is to be on the winning team in the fight between good and evil. The men of the Bible, including Jesus, were both gentle and strong. Today's text features an encounter with a hostile and incredibly dangerous force—the commander of God's angel army! This isn't so much an Old Testament glimpse of Jesus as it is a cool look at God's aggressive side. *Read today's text.*

Can you believe this angel had his sword drawn on the good guy? Joshua had some experiences parallel to those of Moses. Both took their shoes off on holy ground, both commanded the Israelite men to be circumcised, and both took the people through a body of water divinely parted by God in a sort of baptism. Both made war, and that's part of what it means to be a Christian. God is hard core in His wrath upon evil, and when we align ourselves with sin, we align ourselves against God, which, as you can see, is a bad place to be. When we align ourselves with God's call on our lives, however, we are on the winning side of a war—the war for the hearts of mankind.

Which team are you on and why?

_____

_____

_____

_____

_____

_____

_____

_____

_____

_____

_____

_____

_____

_____

The Building Story

—RUTH 1:15–18

Today, we're going to meet Jesus' great-great-great (or something like that) grandmother. Her name is Ruth, and she and her mother-in-law and sister-in-law are now widows. Ruth's mother-in-law Naomi has just told Ruth and Orpah (no, not "Oprah") to just go and start new families, but Ruth is stubborn in the most beautiful way. *Read today's text.*

What would have happened if Ruth had not made this declaration of loyalty? What if she had decided against following Naomi to an unfamiliar country? In the third chapter of the book of Ruth, Ruth and this guy named Boaz (what an awesome name) are married, and their son Obed is born. Ruth, Boaz, and Obed are all named in the genealogy we studied in Matthew 1! Look at how far apart your Bible bookmarks are right now. There are centuries between them. God is writing Jesus' physical family's history, and the story of Ruth is one of its opening chapters. You just met Jesus' ancestors. How cool is that?

What are you passionate about?

_____

_____

_____

_____

_____

_____

_____

_____

_____

_____

_____

_____

_____

Jesus' Life and Ministry

—MATTHEW 9:1–8

The book of Matthew is one of the four Gospels, the books that tell the story of Jesus' life and ministry. The beauty of having four Gospels is that we see four viewpoints on what Jesus said and did. They complement and confirm one another, revealing something new about the event without contradicting the other accounts. *Read today's text.*

The real miracle of this passage is not that Jesus healed a paralyzed man; it is that Jesus looked upon a sinner and proclaimed him forgiven. As He always does, Jesus shows us a physical miracle to illustrate the spiritual miracle for us. Jesus is still in the business of performing that very miracle. May you be like the man in this text who is spiritually paralyzed, brought before Jesus, and proclaimed forgiven. Then, get up and spiritually walk just like the man in this text. Let others be amazed at the healing that Jesus has brought into your life!

How can others see Jesus in you?

41

Fake People

—MATTHEW 9:9–13

You'll notice that we aren't covering every word of Matthew. Part of this is to fit this book's format, but it's also because some of the things we skip in this book will be looked at directly in the follow-up book, *I'm a Christian—Now What?* So, wherever you are on your journey right now, make a note on your bookmarks to get that book when you finish this one. We'll continue exploring the Gospel for those who are new to it, so if you have already given your life to Christ, then you can absolutely keep reading and be blessed, but Day 90 is especially focused on you! *Read today's text.*

When Jesus encountered fake people who claimed to be righteous, He was harsh toward them. When He came to a new place, He went straight to the people who were deepest in sin and ministered lovingly to them right where they were. He loved broken people and called them to leave their lives of sin (John 8:11). A sinner coming to repentance is a huge deal in heaven (Luke 15:7), so Jesus focused His ministry on those who needed Him the most—sinners.

Have you given your life to Christ? If not, why?

_____

_____

_____

_____

_____

_____

_____

_____

_____

_____

_____

_____

_____

_____

Faith

—MATTHEW 9:18–31

Today, we are going to see Jesus perform three—arguably four—miracles in what may have been a very short amount of time. He's called in to heal a girl who is near death, is interrupted on His way by a woman's beautiful act of simple faith, goes on to raise this girl likely from the dead, and then . . . well, I'll let you *read today's text* to see.

Faith was an integral part of each of these miracles, and I'm praying literally right now as I write that it's going to be an integral part of your life from here on. Jesus told this woman, who knew that even the most remote form of contact with Him would heal her forever, that her faith made her well. Then, he went on to raise someone essentially from death, and that's exactly what He does when people believe in Him and are saved. Now, these two blind men call Jesus "the Son of David." In case you've forgotten, Jesus was descended from David, the king of Israel (who was descended from Ruth), and to call Jesus "the Son of David" is to believe the Bible's prophecies about the coming Messiah—that's Jesus.

What is faith for you?

_____

_____

_____

_____

_____

_____

_____

_____

_____

_____

_____

_____

_____

Prove It!

—NUMBERS 24:17

Your fast-track bookmark is about to start doing that huge distance jumping thing that the Hulk does. It's also going to start doing that "prove that Jesus is the Messiah" thing that Saul/Paul does in Acts 9:22; 17:3; and 18:28. Do you remember Abraham and God's promise to him? Do you remember Abraham's son Isaac? Well, Isaac had a son named Jacob. *Read today's text.*

Matthew's Gospel was originally written to persuade Jewish people that Jesus was the Messiah. This is why His genealogy starts with Abraham; to draw a line from Abraham to Jesus proved that Jesus was the "Seed" sent from God to save us all (Galatians 3:16). This was also prophesied in Genesis 12:3 and then fulfilled in the first verse of our main book, Matthew 1:1! Now, if you get the chance today, look also at Genesis 22:18 to see how it was fulfilled in Romans 9:5, and Genesis 17:19 and 21:12 to see them fulfilled in Luke 3:34. I know it's a lot of flipping, but it's good for you, puts hair on your chest, and proves the Bible's truth.

What did you learn from your Bible flipping?

_____

_____

_____

_____

_____

_____

_____

_____

_____

_____

_____

_____

_____

_____

Fulfillment

—2 SAMUEL 7:12–13

Read today's text. These words were prophesied over David, and I don't think he fully understood them in his day. How could he know what his partial descendant Jesus would be like centuries later? Check out this other similar prophecy from Isaiah 9:7, "The dominion will be vast, and its prosperity will never end. He will reign on the throne of David and over his kingdom, to establish and sustain it with justice and righteousness from now on and forever." Whoa. So, not only will this conquering Messiah be descended from King David, but this Messiah's throne will never end! Just imagine how hard this was to read for those who lived in Israel in the centuries after it was written, centuries in which Israel was conquered multiple times.

Now, check out the fulfillment of both today's text and Isaiah 9:7 in Luke 1:32–33 and Romans 1:3. What you're looking at is the fulfillment (New Testament) of prophecies that were written several centuries before (Old Testament).

Have you seen Jesus fulfill things in your life?

_____

_____

_____

_____

_____

_____

_____

_____

_____

_____

_____

_____

_____

John

—MATTHEW 11:1–15

The awesome passages in chapter 10 will be covered in the follow-up book to this one, *I'm a Christian—Now What?* In Isaiah 40:3–5, which is centuries older than Matthew, it was prophesied that a messenger would prepare the way for the Messiah. The Old Testament's age protects us from "circular reasoning." It is not just that the Bible proves the Bible, but that history proves how the Bible has proven itself. Isaiah 40:3–5 is fulfilled in *today's text*.

Yep, that crazy man is John the Baptist. It's not that "Baptist" is his last name; it's that he was baptizing people for the repentance of their sins in preparation for the Messiah who was just around the corner. He's a wild man, and Jesus praises him as the greatest man of all (verse 11). As great as John the Baptist was, though, Jesus said he had nothing on the "lowest" ("least") person in heaven. Think about how awesome heaven is, then! This prophecy about Jesus' forerunner is also fulfilled in Luke 3:3–6, if you want to check that out.

How was John the Baptist both great and the "lowest"?

God Is Drawing Your Heart

—MATTHEW 11:16–19

What if you finish this book without coming to know Christ? I hope to lay out the gospel from various scriptural angles, to introduce you to Jesus from the beginning of the Bible to its end, and to show how ancient prophecies were perfectly fulfilled in the significantly less ancient Gospel of Matthew. Finishing this book and continuing to reject the gospel means you will have turned down one hundred opportunities to respond to the Holy Spirit's drawing through the Scriptures, and I believe that's a big deal. I believe you're holding this book because God is drawing on your heart to be saved. With this in mind, *read today's text*.

Jesus is comparing His generation to a bunch of kids who just won't be pleased. They called John the Baptist "possessed" and Jesus "a drunkard." In the next five verses, He rightfully slams the cities in which He performed miracles because the people there still didn't believe even after the miracles. They blew their every chance. Will you?

Have you decided for Christ?

God's Wrath

—MATTHEW 11:20–24

God's judgment has been poured out on wicked cities in numerous ways. The people of Noah's day were drowned in the flood, refusing to repent after hearing Noah's message (Genesis 7). The cities of Sodom and Gomorrah were consumed with fire from heaven after the people refused to repent (Genesis 19; Romans 1). The cities throughout Canaan were conquered by the Israelite army after the people refused to repent of the most terrible acts imaginable for four hundred years (Leviticus 18; Joshua 11). There are even prophecies in Revelation about God's wrath upon those whom God knows will not repent even after hearing the truth from His two empowered witnesses (Revelation 11). *Read today's text.*

These cities are getting the same prophecy of God's coming wrath for their lack of repentance, only it is specifically because Jesus performed so many miracles in them. Because God's wrath is real and because you and I are sinful, we need to confess that Jesus is Lord and repent from sin!

Are you sinful? What can you do about it?

_____

_____

_____

_____

_____

_____

_____

_____

_____

_____

_____

_____

_____

Are You Convinced?

—PSALM 2:7

As you can see, your fast-track bookmark has jumped forward considerably today. Welcome to the Psalms! This book is way cool: it's a huge collection of songs you can sing to God while playing a banjo, shredding a heavy metal guitar, or drumming on your neighbor's chimney. They were written over the course of many years ranging around a thousand years before Jesus was born. *Read today's text.*

This is an amazing prophecy about Jesus, and you have already read the passage in which it is fulfilled! Go pay a visit back to Matthew 3:16–17, and you'll see that God calls Jesus His Son just as today's text prophesied centuries earlier! You'll begin to see through the fast-track part of this book that one of Matthew's main purposes in writing his Gospel was to convince people that Jesus was the Messiah, the One of whom the Old Testament Scriptures foretold. I hope that you're convinced. This is Matthew's purpose. It is also the purpose of these prophecies.

What was Matthew's purpose?

_____

_____

_____

_____

_____

_____

_____

_____

_____

_____

_____

_____

_____

_____

The Anointed One

—PSALM 21:1–12

Forget about proving that we could only come to exist by a Creator and that our universe's beautiful sense of order could only have come about through design. Prove that the Bible's prophecies about the Messiah are fulfilled in Jesus, and everything else falls into place. Today, we look at the first of a series of passages in the Old Testament which we know were written centuries before Jesus walked the earth yet are fulfilled in Jesus alone.

"The Anointed One" refers to the Messiah at multiple points throughout the Bible, and "Zion" refers to both physical Israel and metaphysical (beyond physical) heaven. The word *consecrated* means that God set Jesus apart, and verse 3 is spoken by those who reject Jesus. What you are about to read was written by David (Acts 4:24–26), but you will see the beautiful things it teaches us about Jesus centuries. It says the Anointed One will be despised (verse 2), the Son of God (verse 7), and ultimately victorious (verses 8–12). *Read today's text.*

What does *consecrated* mean?

_____

_____

_____

_____

_____

_____

_____

_____

_____

_____

_____

_____

_____

_____

Trust in God

—MATTHEW 11:28–30

To be a Christian is to trust in God no matter what, to become aware of one's own sins, to take up one's cross, and to go to war for the gospel . . . but it's also to know the Great Comforter. *Read today's text.*

God expects much from the sinners He redeemed by the blood of His Son, and He has incredible plans of paradise that are beyond your dreams. In the meantime, we are subject to the attacks of evil, the weight of temptation, the consequences of sin, and the pains that come with this life on earth. You need Jesus. You need the rest for your soul that only He provides. The word *yoke* refers to the thing that goes over the shoulders of an ox to make it pull things. We all have some sort of yoke, and Jesus says that His is light. To be a Christian is to have the perfect rest that comes only from Him. Anything else is temporary. The kind of peace the Christian has is bigger than circumstances, heartache, and past failures. It is perfect healing, perfect peace.

How can you trust in God today?

_____

_____

_____

_____

_____

_____

_____

_____

_____

_____

_____

_____

_____

Anger

—MATTHEW 12:9–14

Read today's text. Mark 3:5 and Luke 6:6–11 give us additional insight into this miracle. Did you know that Jesus was *angry* as He performed this miracle? It's true. He was angry with the Pharisees' stubborn hearts when He healed this man. When I stub my toe on a toy at 3:00 a.m. as I'm running to Asher's crib because he's crying, the pain in my toe makes me . . . less than Mickey-Mouse-happy. I get angry. I don't lose my temper often, but when I do, I sometimes have to apologize to people for what I did in my anger. When Jesus got angry here, however, He healed a guy. It's amazing!

When Jesus healed people, there was more going on than just the healing itself. These miracles teach us about God's heart. Think now on something we talked about before. Think about God's wrath upon evil. It's a good thing that God has wrath and gets angry because God's the Good Guy and the bad guys lose. Let God's righteous anger and this healing teach you more about the heart of God.

How do you act when you get angry?

_____

_____

_____

_____

_____

_____

_____

_____

_____

_____

_____

_____

_____

Keep It a Secret

—MATTHEW 12:15–21

Jesus is on this huge healing marathon again in today's text, but He's telling people to keep the whole thing a secret. He didn't shout in the streets to gather a crowd but did the opposite and tried not to draw attention to His healing ministry. He came to do more than heal a few peoples' physical ailments. He came to heal countless more people from the ailment of sin and its eternal consequence of hell. This gentle modesty of Jesus' was prophesied in Isaiah 42:1–4, and that passage is quoted in *today's text*.

In verse 20, you are that injured plant (the bruised reed), and the imagery being conveyed here is of Jesus being so lovingly delicate with your heart. You are that candle that is about to burn out (the smoldering wick), and He will not put you out. When we are overwhelmed and broken, God is gentle with us. Psalm 51:17 and Isaiah 57:15 show us that, when our spirits are broken and our hearts are humbled, God is compassionately pleased with us in that moment. So, in accordance with verse 21, won't you put your hope in Jesus today?

Where have you put your hope?

Unstoppable Joy

—PSALM 45:6–7

The Christian's joy is unstoppable. It is, by its nature, something beyond the temporary pain, trials, wounds, and even difficulties of life. This is the nature of the Messiah's joy as well as of His throne—unstoppable. Daniel 2:44 reads, "In the days of those kings, the God of heaven will set up a kingdom that will never be destroyed, and this kingdom will not be left to another people. It will crush all these kingdoms and bring them to an end, but will itself endure forever." These unstoppable prophecies made centuries before their fulfillments are unmistakable. *Read today's text*.

When we read Luke 1:33 and Hebrews 1:8–12, we see more text proving this prophecy of Psalm 45:6–7 fulfilled, but we see it somewhere else, too. We will see it to be true as Jesus Christ, the Messiah prophesied in the Old Testament and described in the New Testament, returns. This is what it means to be a Christian: it is to believe in both of Christ's arrivals, the one that has happened and the one yet to come!

What does it mean to be a Christian?

_____

_____

_____

_____

_____

_____

_____

_____

_____

_____

_____

_____

_____

Messianic Prophecies

—ISAIAH 7:14–17

The messianic prophecies I've shared with you so far were all spoken in the Old Testament and fulfilled in the New Testament, which makes it easy to see the validity of both the prophecy and the New Testament since it is a widely established fact even amongst people who hate Christianity that the Old Testament is older than the New Testament (go figure). Today's text, however, is both written and fulfilled in Old Testament days. It's also a triple header with three prophecies in a few verses and all of them have been fulfilled. *Read today's text.*

Sure enough, as seen in 2 Kings 18:13 and evidenced in archaeology, the Assyrians came just as Isaiah prophesied they would years before (verse 17). Also, we see Jesus' virgin birth prophesied in verse 14 and fulfilled in Matthew 1:22–23 (which we have read together) as well as in Luke 1:26–31. These alone are enough, but there's also verse 14's prophecy that He would be called "Immanuel" fulfilled in Matthew 1:23! Check my work, and you'll see it's legit! Jesus is the Messiah, and the Bible is true!

What do these fulfilled prophecies mean to you?

_____

_____

_____

_____

_____

_____

_____

_____

_____

_____

_____

_____

_____

_____

Hardened Hearts

—MATTHEW 13:10–17

Matthew is a fulfilled-prophecy-producing machine! The dude is at it again today. Also, have you wondered why Jesus speaks in parables? He answers that very question in *today's text*.

Isaiah 6:9–10 prophesied that people, like most of the Pharisees, would hear Jesus speak but not get His message, or see what Jesus did but refuse to believe their eyes. Do you remember what we read about people's hearts being hardened? The Pharisees were like that, but here we see in verse 15 that God wanted their callous hearts to soften and wanted to cure them if they would only repent. In verse 17, Jesus puts something awesome into perspective for His disciples, and it applies to us as well. For thousands of years throughout the whole Old Testament, prophets of God and righteous people ached to see the Messiah and hear His words. They died in their torturous curiosity, but you are holding in your hands right now a book of the words of the One on whom they waited. Look at how insanely blessed you are. Don't let it go to waste.

List four truths you've learned about Jesus.

_____

_____

_____

_____

_____

_____

_____

_____

_____

_____

_____

_____

_____

_____

A Desperate Father

—MATTHEW 13:31–35

The desperate father who came to Jesus in Mark 9 after Jesus' disciples could not heal his son admitted to Jesus that there was part of him that didn't have faith. Even this admittedly inadequate faith was enough. Jesus takes the smallest seed of faith and grows it into something massive. *Read today's text.*

Boom! So, even the fact that Jesus would speak in parables was another fulfilled messianic prophecy from Psalm 78:2! This first parable is similar to what Jesus will teach later in Matthew 17:20. In this instance, though, it's both a prophecy as to what would happen soon in Jesus' ministry as His few disciples would change the whole world and a picture of someone whose faith helps others to have faith. The second parable is easy to understand when you learn that a yeast cell is super tiny (Google this for an idea: 60 pg [pico=10-12]). Just a little is enough to transform even a big, huge 50-pound bag of flour. Do you have just a little faith? I'll bet it's enough to change your life forever.

How is your faith changing?

Nuts!

—MATTHEW 13:44–46

Read today's text. The guys in these parables know the value of the gospel of Jesus Christ. To them, it is worth everything they have! The first guy in verse 44 sells everything he has when he finds this treasure representing the kingdom of heaven so that he can buy the field it's buried in. Can you imagine what this guy's buddies would say? They would say, "That dude is two crayons short of a full box!" What if you were to give everything you have for the kingdom of heaven? Would people say you're nuts? The guys in these parables don't care because they know it is nothing to give your all in exchange for everything—in exchange for eternity with God. That is what it means to be a Christian!

How can you be nuts for God?

No Good-Looking Pop Star

—ISAIAH 53:1–5

The passage you're about to read was once brought through an office building, and individuals were asked whom this text describes and where it was written. Every one of them answered something like, "That must be Jesus, so it must be in the New Testament." They were correct on the first part, but Isaiah is in the Old Testament. That's right, you're about to read yet another fulfilled prophecy regarding Jesus. As you read, remember that the book of Isaiah is well-known in non-Christian, non-Bible-believing, fully authoritative and scholarly circles to be several centuries older than the Gospels in which we first meet Jesus. *Read today's text.*

Jesus wasn't some good-looking pop star (verse 2). Nothing about Jesus physically drew people to Him, and this was revealed to Isaiah centuries before Jesus' birth. He was rejected by people—even his own family (verse 3). This was also prophesied in Psalm 69:8 and fulfilled in both John 1:11 and John 7:5. Let these prophecies and their fulfillment plant a seed of faith in your heart.

What is your faith revealing?

Mustard Seed

—ISAIAH 53:6–12

Has that seed of faith grown? It doesn't matter how small it is. Do you remember what we read about the mustard seed in Matthew? If you've never seen one, a mustard seed is about the size of the ball at the tip of a ballpoint pen. When you read today's text, I hope that mustard seed-sized faith will grow, and since God can move mountains with a mustard seed-sized faith, just imagine what He can do through you. *Read today's text.*

So, in this prophecy of Isaiah's that is universally known to be hundreds of years older than the Gospel of Matthew, it is said that the Messiah would not open His mouth, though He is led like a lamb to the slaughter (verse 7). Check out Matthew 27:13–14. Boom. Now, verse 9 says that He would take the grave of a rich man after His death. Did you know that Joseph of Arimathea, who owned the tomb into which Jesus' body was laid, was a rich man? Also, verse 12 foretells the Messiah praying for ("interceded" for) the rebels just as Jesus does on the cross centuries later.

What prophecy is fulfilled in today's Scripture?

_____

_____

_____

_____

_____

_____

_____

_____

_____

_____

_____

_____

_____

The End of the World

—MATTHEW 13:47–50

This one is going to be pretty heavy, but I have to share it with you because to skip over it would be dangerous and lousy of me. The last time we read a passage from Matthew, Jesus had just given these parables with this beautiful happy imagery. This one's not happy at all. *Read today's text.*

In verse 49 when Jesus said "the end of the age," He was speaking about what we in our culture have come to call "the end of the world." Here in this parable, He paints a picture of those who are saved being separated from those who are not. Those who are not saved are thrown into a blazing furnace where there is said to be weeping and gnashing (grinding) of teeth. Because Jesus teaches about hell, it's important to know about it. Now, being afraid of hell is not at all what it means to be a Christian, and a fear of hell will not save anyone. Jesus lays this out there because He loves us and does not want anyone to go there. Please read John 3:17; 1 Timothy 2:3–4; and 2 Peter 3:9.

Which will you choose? Heaven or hell?

_____

_____

_____

_____

_____

_____

_____

_____

_____

_____

_____

_____

_____

The Great Commission

—MATTHEW 14:13–16

You're going to love how this book ends. It's so accidentally perfectly timed! It ends on the final command that Jesus gives. This command is famous and is called "The Great Commission." *Read today's text.* When it says, "Jesus had just heard about . . . ," it is referring to John the Baptist's death!

John the Baptist, or "J. to the B." if you want to be 1980's-cool when you talk about him, was beheaded for calling out King Herod the tetrarch (fourth king). When Jesus heard this, He withdrew from the craziness of it all to get away, but a crowd followed Him and, instead of getting upset that His alone time was interrupted, He was filled with compassion for them and healed their sick people (verse 14). Did you see how Jesus took that inadequate amount of fish and bread and multiplied it supernaturally? That's Jesus' style. He takes us, inadequate as we are, and does things through us that are beyond our abilities. This is what it means to be a Christian.

What great things can Jesus do through you? Write them down.

_____

_____

_____

_____

_____

_____

_____

_____

_____

_____

_____

_____

_____

_____

Step of Faith

—MATTHEW 14:14–33

Do you remember our first devotional together? Well, its text is a part of today's devotional. I hope that, after 61 devotionals, you have taken that step of faith off the boat and onto the stormy waters where Jesus may be found, but if you haven't, you are the reason I continue to write. If you have been saved, I hope that all of these messianic prophecies will serve to further convince you of the validity of the gospel and further increase your faith. I hope that you will continue—as Peter does in today's text—to take steps of faith out of your comfort zone and onto the waters toward Jesus. *Read today's text.*

Have courage. Do not be afraid. It is Jesus out there on the waters who calls your name (though Peter asked Jesus to in the text here), and He is Lord over the waters. I pray that you are filled with faith. I pray that whatever would keep you from giving your life to Christ (the waves) would not distract your eyes from your Savior who is steadfastly there for you and unshaken by the waves. I pray Romans 10:9 over you right now.

Have you taken that step? Whom have you told?

_____

_____

_____

_____

_____

_____

_____

_____

_____

_____

_____

_____

_____

Terrified Herod

—JEREMIAH 31:15

We've looked briefly at the dark circumstances surrounding Jesus' birth, and today we will look closer. Jeremiah was a prophet of God whose wealth he gave away more than once and whose words he might have thought went completely to waste. The king to whom he brought his prophecies did not listen, but Jeremiah was really speaking to us. He was speaking to the readers of the greatest selling book of all time. Let Jeremiah speak to you today as you *read today's text.*

Today's text was fulfilled in Matthew 2:16–18, which we haven't read before. This prophecy is tragic but unmistakable. One of the kings named Herod (there were a lot of them) had all the little boys of Bethlehem who were about Jesus' age killed because Herod was terrified at the thought of this little King taking over his throne. The Messiah was born into a story of anguish, but He turned it into one of triumph. To be a Christian is to have your tragedy transformed.

How will you be transformed?

_____

_____

_____

_____

_____

_____

_____

_____

_____

_____

_____

_____

_____

Fulfilled by God

—HOSEA 11:1

The evidence from the Bible that proves Jesus was the prophesied Messiah is so overwhelming in part because many of the prophecies were fulfilled by Jesus in ways that Jesus could not have made happen as an adult. He could not control where He was born, where His parents moved, or who His ancestors were. Jesus was born from the line of Jacob, whose name was Israel and whose grandfather was Abraham. God's promise to Abraham is the basis for the new covenant whereby people are saved no longer by the old covenant, but by believing in Jesus as Lord (Romans 10 and Galatians 3). Today's tiny verse refers directly to the nation of Israel, and its reflection is one of Jesus, God's Son. *Read today's text.*

In Matthew 2:13–15, we see Hosea's words on God's behalf about Israel fulfilled as an uncanny prophecy. God would call Joseph, Mary, and their son out of Egypt. Jesus was too little to just make this prophecy's fulfillment happen on His own. It was fulfilled by God (verse 15).

Do you stand by the clear truths of Scripture and its fulfilled prophecies?

_____

_____

_____

_____

_____

_____

_____

_____

_____

_____

_____

_____

_____

_____

Perfectly Well

—MATTHEW 15:29–31

Go ahead and *read today's text*. I wonder how many people were healed in this passage. It's like those last few verses of chapter 14 wherein people just touched the tassels of Jesus' robe and were made "perfectly well." That's just what Jesus does. These people had the faith that even the slightest contact with Jesus would heal them, and it did. They weren't made partially well or put in better moods.

Their lifelong infirmities were taken away after they came in contact with the Healer. My prayer for you right now is that, as you go throughout your day today, you would be ministered to by the Healer and that your soul would soon be made perfectly well by even this subtle contact with Jesus.

What needs healing in your life?

_____

_____

_____

_____

_____

_____

_____

_____

_____

_____

_____

_____

_____

The Son of Man

—MATTHEW 16:13–17

Before you read today's text, I want you to write on your bookmark in big letters who Jesus is to you. Is He a fascinating historical figure? Is He only a miracle worker, or is He your Lord and Savior? Write it on your bookmark today. It may change in the days to come. *Read today's text.*

Remember, the title "Son of Man" is part of the Old Testament's prophecies about the Messiah, and Jesus identified Himself as the Son of Man. Also, did you catch the names of our boys John the Baptist ("J. to the B.") and Jeremiah in verse 14? People had all sorts of theories because many just didn't quite know what to make of Jesus, but Peter gets it right. Peter gets it right because God the Father revealed it to Him. Wrap your head around that for a moment and see just what a big deal that is. This is what it means to be a Christian: it is to be drawn by God the Father (John 6:44) to see that Jesus is His Son (like Peter in today's text) and then filled with the Holy Spirit (Acts 2:38).

Who is Jesus to you?

An Average Fisherman

—MATTHEW 16:18–20

Peter's relationship with Jesus had its ups and downs, but we are going to see a huge mountain top moment in today's text. Peter was an average Joe fisherman when he was first called to follow Jesus. He made some pretty bonehead moves as a disciple, but God obviously had some big plans for him that were beyond what Peter was capable of himself. *Read today's text.*

Maybe you've been to a really messed up church in the past and now you hold all churches responsible for it. Maybe you went to a great church and then its leadership did something terrible. I can't possibly know your story, but I do know that the overall church itself across the world will not be overcome by Hell itself. Jesus prophesied that over Peter here in today's text and it has proven true for over two millennia so far. If you have not already, I want you to deliberately take some time right now to look into nearby churches that teach a great deal of the Bible each time they meet. Go find an imperfect church and join it today.

What church are you attending or hoping to attend?

_____

_____

_____

_____

_____

_____

_____

_____

_____

_____

_____

_____

_____

_____

68

New and Old Treasures

—MICAH 5:2

The end of Matthew 13, which we skipped, says that a student of Scripture (that's you and me) is like a landowner who brings out new and old treasures. We've been in the New Testament for a few entries, and now it's time to bring out and marvel at another old treasure. *Read today's text and even verses 1–15 if you have time.*

This passage was fulfilled in Matthew 2:1 and Luke 2:4-6. The book of Micah was written almost 900 years before the books of Matthew and Luke. Think about that for a second and think about it in light of the fact that babies cannot control where or when they are born. Also, if you had time to read all fifteen verses of the passage, you saw the prophecies about both the Assyrian invasion of Israel and Yahweh's victory over the Assyrians for Israel's rescue. Turn on the news, or ask your parents' permission to Google the nation of Israel right now. It's still there. This means God delivered it not only from the Assyrians, as He said He would in Micah 5, but from the other nations that would invade in the centuries that followed.

What did you learn about the nation of Israel?

_____

_____

_____

_____

_____

_____

_____

_____

_____

_____

_____

_____

_____

Donkeys

—ZECHARIAH 9:9

When you read today's text, you're going to think to yourself, "Jesse Campbell, you are not the fastest tree in the woods. Why did you have me flip through my Bible for this weird little single verse about donkeys?" Then, you're going to flip to Mark 11:7–11 and immediately know why. *Read today's text and then read Mark 11:7–11.*

How do you like that? The book of Zechariah was written almost six hundred years before the book of Mark was written. Now, before you think that Jesus may have snagged Himself a donkey because He knew about the prophecy in Zechariah that the Messiah would ride in on a donkey, peek ahead to Matthew 21:1–5. Seriously, do it. Yeah, yeah, I know I'm making you flip through the Bible or type into your search bar, but it's worth it! Now, do you see? Write on your bookmark that I have just given you yet another reason to believe that the Bible is true and that Jesus is the Messiah. In Jesus' name, may you see these fulfilled prophecies, be filled with faith, and be saved!

Write down the reason to believe from this devotion.

_____

_____

_____

_____

_____

_____

_____

_____

_____

_____

_____

_____

_____

_____

_____

That Creepy Feeling

—MATTHEW 16:24–28

Have you ever had this creeping feeling in a "new" place that somehow you've been there before? I felt that once when I went to a concert near my state's capital and realized that I had been in that same auditorium ten years before as a kid to receive my state science fair award. Yep, I had a nerdy streak, but I've kept that a secret . . . until now. *Read today's text.*

Did you get that creepy feeling? You should have because we read this verse in the second devotional of this book! Today, you read it in *context,* though. To read something in context is to read everything that comes before it and everything that comes after it. Christians stand by the Bible, and they do it not just because they have picked out a few words they like, but because they know their passage's *context.* This passage brings us back to what it means to be a Christian: it is to take up the ultimate device of selflessness and follow Jesus. Because we'll all be judged by God (verse 27), why would it matter in that moment that we *had* a lot of stuff while alive (verse 26)?

What does it mean to you to be a Christian?

Creepy Weird Stuff

—MATTHEW 17:14–21

Today, we'll get into the creepy weird stuff of Christianity. Jesus is about to cast a demon out of a boy. Yeah, it's intense. Now, the real focus of the passage is not so much the demon as it is the boys' father and his faith, so I want you to read this passage as well as its parallel in the Gospel of Mark 9:17–29. So, along with that passage from Mark, *read today's text*.

My son Aiden suffered in a way similar to this boy. Because Aiden was born without a windpipe, he could not speak and would sometimes develop foam around his mouth. I asked everyone I knew to both pray and ask everyone they knew to pray that my Aiden would be healed. As a result, God did the impossible (verse 20).

Do you have faith like the father in this passage? Buddy, I desperately hope that you would come to believe. If you believe, even with the faith of a tiny mustard seed, you can move the mountains in your life! Nothing will be impossible for you!

Where do you put your faith?

A Bunch of Goobers

—MATTHEW 18:1–14

The disciples were a bunch of goobers. They got into dumb arguments all the time. In Matthew 17:22–23, Jesus just told them for the second time at this point that He was going to be crucified and rise again, which was the biggest prophecy Jesus made (something they would prove to have forgotten after the crucifixion), and now they're in an argument over who is the best. Ugh. *Read today's text.*

Jesus tells them they must be converted and become like children, or they will never enter the kingdom of heaven (verse 3). I hope you caught that, because it applies to you and me. In verse 8, Jesus reprises a teaching He gave in the Sermon on the Mount and ties it into this beautiful and challenging call to be childlike in our faith. Write the word *childlike* on your hand right now. Go ahead. I'll wait. Each time you see that today, I want you to remember this passage because I believe that God is going to use it to teach you its meaning today. Be converted. Trust God the way my crazy children trust me. This is what it means to be a Christian!

Write down "childlike faith." What does that mean?

_____

_____

_____

_____

_____

_____

_____

_____

_____

_____

_____

_____

_____

_____

400 Years Later

—MALACHI 4:1–6

Whoa! Our fast-track bookmark is heading for the last verse of the Old Testament today! Write a note on it about that now. Before you read today's text, you have to know that God did not inspire anyone to write something on His behalf for four hundred years after these words! It's like leaving everyone in this excruciating state of suspense for four centuries. Now, to see if you have been paying attention, as you read, try to name the one who fulfills this prophecy. *Read today's text.*

This prophecy was fulfilled a few chapters ago in our progress through Matthew in chapter 11 verses 7–15 and in 17:10–13. This "Elijah" is J. to the B.! It's John the Baptist! Did you know that countless God-loving people waited four centuries to learn what you just read? Now, this idea of a forerunner going before the One will come back toward the end of our devotionals together. Satan will take this idea and imitate it. He will put his own sort of J. to the B. before the Antichrist. You see, the Bible has mostly fulfilled prophecies, but some have yet to be fulfilled.

Who fulfills the prophecy from today's verse?

_____

_____

_____

_____

_____

_____

_____

_____

_____

_____

_____

_____

_____

Welcome to the New Testament

—ROMANS 6:20–23

Write a note on your fast-track bookmark welcoming it into the New Testament! Also, write on it that you've seen more than twenty Old Testament prophecies about the Messiah along with their corresponding fulfill-ments in the New Testament. Isn't the Bible amazing? Now, your fast-track bookmark has just skipped your Matthew bookmark and a book titled "Acts." For what may be your first look at the books of the Bible we call "the epistles," *read today's text*.

That last verse is like the whole gospel in a nutshell. The wages of our sin is eternity in hell apart from God, but God offers us this gift that is eternal life in heaven through the transforming belief in Christ! Receive this gift! Believe in Jesus and, drawn by God's Holy Spirit, make Him the Lord of your life! As verses 20 and 21 teach, we have sin in our lives, and that sin leads to death. Because of our sin, we need Jesus!

Draw a picture showing how sin separates us from God.

_____

_____

_____

_____

_____

_____

_____

_____

_____

_____

_____

_____

_____

_____

_____

Where Do You Stand?

—MATTHEW 19:16–26

Write on your Matthew bookmark a follow-up to something we wrote way back on Day 17. Write where you stand with God right now, and as you do, would you be sensitive in your heart to what may be God's drawing upon it to finally be saved if you aren't already? If you want a refresher on how to be saved and don't want to wade through all the messianic prophecy stuff we've been focusing on, please look at yesterday's devotional. *Read today's text.*

This guy thought that his obedience to the law would save him, but the truth is that according to the Old Testament laws no one is righteous enough to be saved! He already had a lord in his life, and that lord was his possessions. It's not that everyone has to deliberately go bankrupt in order to be saved, but this passage does show us that people who do not make Jesus the Lord of their lives and obey His will are not saved. What's the one thing you wouldn't be willing to give up if Jesus asked you to?

What wouldn't you be willing to give up?

Son of David

—MATTHEW 20:29–34

Do you remember what it means to call Jesus "the Son of David"? Because it was prophesied that a descendant of David's would be the Messiah (Psalm 132:11; Isaiah 9:7; and others) and since Jesus was of David's line (Matthew 1:6 and 16), Jesus is "the Son of David" whose ancestry qualifies Him as the Messiah. He's also about to prove that He is the Messiah by working another cool miracle. *Read today's text.*

Did you catch verse 31? Read it again. The crowd shushed these blind men, but the blind men didn't listen, and because the blind men didn't listen, they wouldn't be blind much longer! Make a "T" chart on your bookmark, and on one side write the initials of the people who are like this crowd and would shush you if you started going all Christian on them. Then write the initials of the people who would be stoked if you started going all Christian like these *formerly* blind men in today's text. Sometimes being a Christian means shouting over the shushers.

What can you say to people who want you to keep quiet about Jesus?

_____

_____

_____

_____

_____

_____

_____

_____

_____

_____

_____

_____

_____

You're Busted

—MATTHEW 21:1–11

Read today's text. That's an interesting passage, right? It's totally new, and you've never read it before, right? No! You're busted! If this passage seems new to you, then you haven't been looking up the passages I've given you in parentheses that show how those messianic prophecies we saw in the Old Testament were fulfilled in the New Testament! (Sigh . . .) It's okay. We can still be buddies, but I want you to look up every cross reference I give you.

We've just entered a really cool chapter of the Bible. The word "Hosanna" means "God, come save us." Apparently, the children in the city (which verse 10 says was shaken by Jesus' arrival) heard the crowds shouting this because they start shouting it, too, in verses 14–17. Sadly, though, some of the people who were hyped for Jesus' arrival were later hyped to see Him crucified. Their excitement for meeting Jesus was short-lived. Being a Christian means more than just being hyped for a little while.

What can you be hyped about for your entire life?

_____

_____

_____

_____

_____

_____

_____

_____

_____

_____

_____

_____

_____

Truly Amazing

—GALATIANS 4:4–7

This passage is going to be overwhelming and beautiful if you understand it. It's truly amazing. The laws of the Old Testament show us how far we fall from God's standards as we saw when we studied Jesus' Sermon on the Mount in Matthew chapters 5–7. With that in mind, *read today's text.*

Verse 4 is connected to Genesis 3:15 and Matthew 1:20. It's so amazing that we would say to the holy, omnipotent, in-charge, Creator-Judge the word "Abba," which means "Daddy." It's amazing because you and I have sin, and sin makes us unworthy of even the presence of our perfect God. Though we are sinful, God the Father sent God the Son to meet us eye-to-eye under the law (verse 5) to offer us adoption that we might be called sons of God alongside Jesus (John 1:12). We are no longer slaves to sin with our hopeless efforts to obey the law (Isaiah 64:6; Romans 7:7–25; Hebrews 10:1–7). Now we are adopted sons of the King! Because of what Jesus did through His resurrection after the cross, we sinners can look to God and call Him "Daddy!"

Why can you call God "Daddy"?

The Flesh

—GALATIANS 5:19–26

Read today's text. It's our conceit that leads us to crave the status of those "above" us (verse 26). It's our sin nature, which we all inherited from Adam, that leads us to the negative things described in verses 19–21. This sin nature is called "the flesh" here. As the father of multiple sons under the age of four, I can attest to the fact that babies are born with black belts in sin: it is godliness that must be taught to them because disobedience and sin come *quite* naturally to all of us in our flesh.

Remember that "fruit" is what is produced by something or someone because of its or his nature (see Matthew 7:15–29, which we read on Day 35), and the fruit of the Holy Spirit of God, who draws, convicts, lives in, and then empowers Christians, is "love, joy, peace, patience, kindness, goodness, faith, gentleness, and self-control" (verses 22–23). If you are saved and therefore have the Holy Spirit of God in you, then these fruits will result. If you do not show these fruits by the power of the Holy Spirit and do not repent from sin, then you aren't saved (Romans 8:6–11).

What fruit is your life producing?

_____

_____

_____

_____

_____

_____

_____

_____

_____

_____

_____

_____

_____

_____

A Parable

—MATTHEW 21:28–32

True to His teaching style, which was prophetically described centuries ahead of time in Psalm 78:2 as well as Isaiah 6:9–10 and explained in Matthew 13:10–17, which we studied on Day 55, Jesus is using a parable to teach in *today's text*.

So, the first son refused to do what the father asked him to but eventually did it, and the second son said that he would do the father's will but never actually followed through. Jesus asks the Pharisees which of the two sons actually does the father's will, and their correct answer in verse 31 validates their terrible guilt all the more: they unknowingly admitted to being the second son. In their pride, they bragged about how righteous they were, but they did not do the will of God and did not recognize God Himself when He stood in front of them in Jesus' flesh. They were all talk and no follow-through. They were all show and no go. So, though they dressed in the best clothes and said loudly the best things (Luke 18:9–14), they weren't saved.

Which of the two sons in Matthew 21:28–32 will you be?

_____

_____

_____

_____

_____

_____

_____

_____

_____

_____

_____

_____

_____

_____

Posing as a Christian

—MATTHEW 22:1–14

The Jewish authorities were expecting the Messiah to lead a Jewish revolt to kick the Romans out of Israel, but Jesus had mostly harsh things to say about the Jewish leadership and even told them that their city Jerusalem would be overtaken and that non-Jewish people (Gentiles) would be saved. In both chapter 21 and here, Jesus calls the Jewish authorities out for killing the prophets God sent to them over the years and for now preparing to kill the sent Son of God. This parable uses a king to symbolize God, the king's slaves to symbolize the prophets of God, and the diverse mix of people on the outskirts of town to symbolize the Gentiles. *Read today's text.*

This guy at the wedding isn't doing what you do or wearing what you wear when you go to a wedding and has nothing to say in his defense is like the people described in Matthew 7:21–23: the person posing as a Christian and not actually doing the will of God. If you have been invited and belong to God (verse 14), if you are truly saved, you are going to do God's will.

What is God's will for your life?

_____

_____

_____

_____

_____

_____

_____

_____

_____

_____

_____

_____

_____

_____

Thou Shalts

—MATTHEW 22:34–40

Here it is—the ultimate answer to the question about all the "thou shalts" of the Bible! Today we read the commands of the Bible boiled down to two simple commands, and the chef doing the boiling is Jesus Himself! *Read today's text.*

This question was set as a trap. The Pharisees (Jewish religious leaders) would sometimes offer Jesus door number 1 and door number 2. Each "door" would have some trap behind it, but Jesus would always see through their intentions and make for Himself door number 3, and it would leave everyone's mind blown. So, here is Jesus' brilliant and, of course, perfect answer: love. Love God with all of your heart, soul, and mind. Love your neighbor the way you love yourself. This is what it means to be a Christian! It means to love God with all of your thought-out emotions, your very being, and with everything your mind is capable of! Next, it is to love yourself and love others just as much!

How can you love your neighbor?

_____

_____

_____

_____

_____

_____

_____

_____

_____

_____

_____

_____

Binocular Time!

—1 TIMOTHY 1:12–17

All right, let's put on our binoculars here. Let's suppose that, even though you may have read 82 devotionals from a book whose author (that's me, my name is Jesse, and I love you) is trying to lead you to be saved, you are still not a Christian. If that's you, then you might have a hard time envisioning this, but you also might find the idea amazing. For more on this, definitely get the next book, titled *I'm a Christian—Now What?*, because we face this question in that book from time to time. Are you called to be a minister? *Read today's text.*

Here, Paul lays out the fact that he was completely unqualified to be a minister. He gives all the credit to the mercy of Christ Jesus (verse 16). He knew that God would use him as an example for others to show just how far God's reach is: Paul was once way too far lost to be considered a future minister, yet he became one of the best known apostles in history. So, no matter how far you've been from God, God can use you. Don't write off the possibility of becoming a full-time minister.

How can God use you? Dream big!

Get in Church

—LUKE 3

Have you been going to church like I challenged you to several devotions ago? I hope so! Get in church, dude! Today, *skim through Luke 3, or read the whole thing. Either way, check out the last name in verse 33.*

This prophecy that Jesus would be descended from Judah (the dude; not the tribe named "Judah") appears way back in Genesis 49:10 near the beginning of the Bible and pops up elsewhere like in Hebrews 7:14. I wanted you at least to get a glimpse into Luke's Gospel—the opening chapter, to see that he was inspired to provide a genealogy, too, only one that's different from Matthew's. Matthew wrote mostly to convince Jews that Jesus is the Messiah, but Luke had Gentiles in mind. The Holy Spirit inspired them both to make sure everyone's heart would be spoken to directly. That's the last messianic prophecy we're going to look at. From here on, we're focusing on your heart.

How has your heart been spoken to?

_____

_____

_____

_____

_____

_____

_____

_____

_____

_____

_____

_____

_____

What Does It Mean?

—MATTHEW 23:25–28

What does it mean to be a Christian? Does it mean doing and saying the right things? Does it mean looking the best you possibly can on the outside while your heart is far from God? No, this was the approach taken by the Pharisees whom Jesus is telling off in the first part of Matthew 23. He is calling them out for focusing on appearances, exalting themselves, and oppressing others who just want to worship God. *Read today's text.*

Harsh words, huh? Notice Jesus' imagery with the cup in verse 25 and the tomb in verse 27. Their outsides were clean, but their insides were dirty and dead. God cares more about having your heart than He cares about how well you can keep your act together in front of other people. He cares more about your heart than your obedience to His commands because He knows that, if He has your heart, your obedience will flow from that. To have a godly appearance but a heart that rebels against God—this is what it means to be one of these Pharisees. To have a heart that is fully God's—this is what it means to be a Christian.

List what it means to you to be a Christian.

_____

_____

_____

_____

_____

_____

_____

_____

_____

_____

_____

_____

_____

Look at Your Heart

—MATTHEW 23:37–39

That you've made it this far into this book must mean that God is really drawing on your heart to be saved. We've begun to look at your heart, but let's also get a glimpse of God's heart in *today's text*.

I wonder if Jesus had tears in His eyes as He shouted this! Look at how much He cares for the people of Jerusalem—the very same people He just told off for 36 verses! He wanted to draw them near, but they were not willing (verse 37). Is that you? Are you being drawn by God to be saved but are pushing back (Acts 7:51)? In Jesus' name, be saved. Drawn by the Holy Spirit, confess with your mouth out loud right there where you sit (I don't care who hears), "Jesus is Lord," and know by faith in your heart that Jesus is the Son of God (John 3:16) who is the only way to be saved (John 14:6), who died for your sins (Romans 3:23), and who rose again from the dead (Romans 10:9)! This is how someone is saved. This is what it means to be a Christian!

Write down what you confess!

_____

_____

_____

_____

_____

_____

_____

_____

_____

_____

_____

_____

_____

_____

My Student

—MATTHEW 24:1–2, 29–31

If you've been drawn by the Holy Spirit to confess with your mouth that Jesus is Lord and believe in your heart that God raised Him from the dead, then put this book down and tell your parents or guardian(s) that you want to be baptized! If not, read yesterday's devotional again. Be saved by God's grace. Be saved because Jesus is coming back again. In *today's text*, we'll see some prophecies about the end of the age of the church as the disciples knew it and the end of the world as we know it.

In the year 70, the Romans attacked Jerusalem. Convinced there was treasure in its walls, they disassembled the temple brick by brick, and Jesus' prophecy in verse 2 was fulfilled. Verses 29–31, however, are prophecies that have yet to be fulfilled! With all of the fulfilled prophecies we've seen, don't you know that God will fulfill these as well? To live one's life inspired by the fact that Jesus is coming back is a big part of what it means to be a Christian.

How will you live inspired?

_____

_____

_____

_____

_____

_____

_____

_____

_____

_____

_____

_____

_____

What's the Point?

—1 PETER 1:3–9

What is the point of faith? Salvation. The goal in having faith is to be saved. By grace through faith, may your heart belong to Christ and your soul be saved (Ephesians 2:8). To be a Christian is to suffer and know all the while that God is good and that your faithful love for God is being made stronger. Peter, the one who walked on water in that step of faith that we saw earlier, is the one whom Jesus said would be the rock-solid foundation for the church (Matthew 16:18). The Rock (not the wrestler/actor dude, but the disciple of Jesus dude) wrote to the churches around Rome who were suffering for their Christian faith. *Read today's text.*

These Christians were being hunted by their crazy emperor Nero, and Christians were being killed in brutal ways. The church met in secret places, and they suffered greatly. However, the first members grew stronger against the wind, and the church you go to today can trace its roots to the earliest Christians.

How did Peter step out in faith? How will you?

_____

_____

_____

_____

_____

_____

_____

_____

_____

_____

_____

_____

_____

To Be a Christian

—1 PETER 1:13–16

If you haven't yet given your life to Christ, please review the opening devotions of this book and speak with a pastor about how to be saved! The remaining devotions will be directed to brand new Christians, and I sure hope you're reading them as someone who's learning what it means to be a Christian not just from a devotional book, but from experience! *Read today's text.*

To be a Christian is to be a sinner who craves holiness. Our hearts inherited our sinful nature from Adam. That's heavy news because God is the ultimate Embodiment of absolute holiness. We sinful young men cannot dare approach God because of His intense holiness. In Exodus 33:20, God told Moses that no living sinful person could see Him and live! So, Jesus, whose miraculous birth kept Him from inheriting our sin nature, made a way for sinful man to be with holy God. Jesus lived a holy life, and now we are called to be holy (verse 16 and much of Leviticus). We're also called to set our hope *completely* on Jesus' return (verse 13)!

Write down any questions you have, and then talk to an adult about them.

_____

_____

_____

_____

_____

_____

_____

_____

_____

_____

_____

_____

_____

What's Your Date?

—MATTHEW 25:31–46

Write on your Matthew bookmark in the boldest letters of all your entries the date you gave your life to Christ. We're going to do something cool with your bookmarks soon. Today's parable is both a frightening teaching about those who rejected Christ being cast from His presence and a beautifully convicting teaching about God's heart for the poor. *Read today's text*.

Over and over, Jesus calls us to look after poor people. They hold a special place in God's heart and should hold one in ours as well. In Matthew 7:21, we saw that it's not those who only say the right things who are saved, but those who *do* God's will *because* they know God and are saved. In this passage, it's clearly shown that doing God's will includes caring for the poor. Caring for the poor is the same thing as caring for God Himself. Even poor people whose situations are their own fault can be helped. After all, that's how God ministers to us. Pray that you would one day hear the words of verse 34.

How can you help the poor?

_____

_____

_____

_____

_____

_____

_____

_____

_____

_____

_____

_____

_____

The Lord's Supper

—MATTHEW 26:17–35

Read today's text. Wow. Jesus reclined and ate with His disciples knowing about the betrayal (verse 21). In John 13, we see another event that took place at this same supper. Knowing Judas was going to betray Him, Jesus washed all of His disciples' feet and said that we should do the same (John 13:1–2 and verse 14). Notice the disciples' passionate declarations of loyalty to Jesus (verse 35). Even Judas denies Jesus' prediction!

The meal they're eating is a special meal eaten in memory of the Passover in Moses' time, when the blood of a lamb was smeared over the doorpost of a Hebrew family's house to spare them from the final plague of Egypt—the death of the house's firstborn son. This dress rehearsal for the first Communion was the moment the Passover meal pivoted into the new covenant and became Communion as we know it today. Being a Christian includes taking Communion. Pray and ready yourself for your next opportunity to take the Lord's Supper at church.

What will you remember the next time you take the Lord's Supper?

_____

_____

_____

_____

_____

_____

_____

_____

_____

_____

_____

_____

_____

_____

Deserted

—MATTHEW 26:47–56

Read today's text. So, the disciples who just promised to stay loyal to Jesus until death in yesterday's devotional have all deserted Him in today's devotional (verse 56). Judas just betrayed Jesus! This, too, was prophesied. In our culture today, people can put this official stamp on their friendship by becoming "friends" online. In Jesus' culture, people's friendships were made official by breaking bread together. Jesus and Judas had just broken bread together, making this betrayal all the more painful for Jesus even though Jesus saw it coming (Psalm 41:9).

Verse 53 reveals something *awesome* about Jesus. He could have had twelve legions of angels come to His aid at any moment, but He never called them. There were six thousand troops in a legion, so twelve legions would have been seventy-two thousand angels kicking tail and delivering Jesus! The nails did not keep Jesus on the cross. He could have ended things at any point. No, it was His prophesied quest to glorify the Father and His love for you that kept Him there.

Write out your prayer of thanks to your Savior.

_____

_____

_____

_____

_____

_____

_____

_____

_____

_____

_____

_____

_____

Behold the Lamb

—REVELATION 13 AND 19:11–21

At the end of the world, the Antichrist (portrayed by the first beast in Revelation 13:1–10) takes over the world's political scene and has the world worship him. He has this guy who goes before him (the second beast in verses 11–18). This is Satan's twisted mockery of Jesus' ministry being proclaimed ahead of time by John the Baptist. Darkly similar to the way that John the Baptist said, "Behold the Lamb of God who takes away the sins of the world," this second beast will perform miracles to cause the world to worship the Antichrist. Satan has no creativity; all he can do is imitate. *Read Revelation 13.*

Things look bleak at the end of Revelation 13, but never doubt that your Savior is unconquerable! *Read Revelation 19:11–21.* As we just read yesterday, Jesus' first coming culminated in this incredible act of pacifism (not fighting), but His second coming will culminate in this glorious victory over evil! Believing this and living in light of it are part of what it means to be a Christian.

Why do you think Satan tries to mock Jesus?

_____

_____

_____

_____

_____

_____

_____

_____

_____

_____

_____

_____

_____

_____

Final Battle Royale

—REVELATION 20:7–10

Today's text is what makes it possible to face life's difficulties. It's crucial to understanding God's heart even when things seem hopeless. It's also the most horrifying thing to Satan. On Day 18, we studied Genesis 3:15 wherein God prophesied His victory over Satan directly to the snake—Satan himself. It was part of Day 78, too, and now we see how this prophecy will be fulfilled in Revelation. Remember that the Antichrist is called "the beast," his forerunner is the false prophet, and Satan is the dragon. *Read today's text.*

The absolute best "final battle royale" scenes of today's greatest superhero movies all combined would have nothing on what the moment described in this text will be like. In that moment, everything that ever went wrong in your life will be made right. Satan will answer for everything he has done and be annihilated! So, though now we may suffer, we know that Jesus wins. Though now we do battle, the war will be won! To be a Christian is to share in that victory!

Who wins the battle? Write it down.

_____

_____

_____

_____

_____

_____

_____

_____

_____

_____

_____

_____

_____

_____

95

Peer Pressure

—MATTHEW 26:69–75

In verse 33, at the Last Supper, Peter promised never to run away even if everyone else did, and Jesus' response in verse 34 is "I assure you, tonight before the rooster crows, you will deny Me three times!" *Read today's text.*

As a Christian, you *cannot* cower to peer pressure the way Peter does here. Peter should have known that he couldn't blend in at the courtyard bonfire (verse 69; Luke 22:55; and Mark 14:54) and at the gateway (verse 71). He even goes so far as to publicly swear with an oath and curse in front of everyone about how he's not a Christian. Look at how far he's fallen. Peter's looking at the waves again, isn't he? As a Christian, you're going to have these rooster-crow moments when the pressure is intense. You may even have moments of doubt, or spiritual failure. If you do, know that God redeems us and will still use us even after failure. Know that to be a Christian is to always be a Christian. In *I'm a Christian—Now What?* we'll study John 21 wherein the resurrected Jesus heals Peter's broken heart. Take a minute to pray now.

Write down your prayer concerning peer pressure.

_____

_____

_____

_____

_____

_____

_____

_____

_____

_____

_____

_____

_____

I'm Transformed

—MATTHEW 27:45–66

Today, we see the cost of our sin. It's tremendous. I've lost a son. My boy Aiden is waiting on us in heaven. My wife and I have lived through this pain, and it taught us to understand better today's text. Our sin cost God His Son. *Read today's text.*

Notice that it went dark at noon (verse 45). In verses 50 and 51 Jesus gave up His spirit as He shouted, "It is finished!" (John 19:30). The curtain was torn that separated the presence of God in the interior of the sanctuary from the people outside. That curtain was a barrier representing Jesus' body, according to Hebrews 10:20; it was broken, and now all who call on the name of the Lord will be saved (Joel 2:32; Acts 2:21; Romans 10:13). According to Mark 15:43 and John 19:38, Joseph of Arimathea was one of the Pharisees, and now he is helping to bury Jesus properly. Review Day 59. What a transformation! To be a Christian is to be transformed. It's to be paid for by the blood of Jesus.

Write on your bookmark, "I'm transformed!"

_____

_____

_____

_____

_____

_____

_____

_____

_____

_____

_____

_____

_____

_____

Happy Easter

—MATTHEW 28:1–15

All of Christianity depends on today's text being true. If the resurrection of Jesus Christ from the dead didn't happen, then we are to be pitied because we believe a lie (1 Corinthians 15). Yesterday, we saw Jesus pay the price for our sin with His death, but today we see Him rise up in victory over it! *Read today's text.*

This is so vitally important that it's worth building your whole life around! It's also provable! That the chief priests and elders would pay the soldiers to lie and claim that Jesus' body had been stolen proves that the tomb was empty! If they could have shown everyone Jesus' dead body, they absolutely would have, and Christianity would have been stopped. Also, all the disciples except John faced terrible deaths and stayed faithful to the fact that they had seen the resurrected Jesus! They went from a bunch of cowardly knuckle-heads to a bunch of Holy-Spirit-filled world changers. Now, go be a world changer because Jesus rose again!

Make a list of people you can tell about Jesus.

_____

_____

_____

_____

_____

_____

_____

_____

_____

_____

_____

_____

_____

A Mind-Blowing Story

—ACTS 1:1–11

All right, it's arts and crafts time. Take your Matthew bookmark and lay it out long-ways vertically in front of you. Now, take your fast-track bookmark and lay it horizontally across your Matthew bookmark a few inches from the top. Fasten them together laminated, framed, or whatever works. The two bookmarks make a cross that's covered with glimpses of your testimony— the story of how you became a Christian! It will make a beautiful tool as you share your story with others. *Read today's text.*

The resurrected Jesus just ascended to heaven and told His remaining disciples that they would receive the Holy Spirit and spread the news about His resurrection all over the world (verse 8). Whoa! Welcome to the book of Acts! This is the mind-blowing story of how the church was born. Yes, the church has its origins in the book of Acts—I guarantee it. The whole thing starts with the ascension (rising up) of Jesus to heaven and then the coming down of the Holy Spirit.

What does reading your bookmarks say to you?

_____

_____

_____

_____

_____

_____

_____

_____

_____

_____

_____

_____

_____

What's Gotten into Peter?

—ACTS 2:1–33

You will never believe what's gotten into Peter since Jesus' resurrection. *Read today's text.*

A violent rushing wind? Fire from heaven causing people to hear untaught foreigners speaking their own languages? Peter, whom we last saw cowering at the accusations of a servant girl, now speaking boldly to a crowd of thousands? They must all be drunk. Oh, wait, no . . . they're not (verse 15). This Holy Spirit is the Advocate Jesus prophesied would come after He ascended to heaven (John 16:7). He draws us to be saved, dwells in us upon salvation, and comes upon us to do amazing things. We encounter the Holy Spirit together as a church through worship and Bible study. We worship filled with the Holy Spirit, and we live our lives guided by this same Holy Spirit from today's text. To be a Christian is to be filled with the Holy Spirit, and to lack the Holy Spirit is to not be a Christian yet (Romans 8:9–10)! What's gotten into Peter? The Holy Spirit of God has.

What's gotten into you?

Take Up Your Cross

—MATTHEW 28:16–20

On Day 2, we saw that to be a Christian is to take up your cross daily and follow Jesus. Now, you have a cross made from your bookmarks that is covered with pieces of your testimony, and you are going to take that cross up everyday in your heart and share your testimony with others. What does it mean to be a Christian? *It means to make other Christians! Read today's text.*

This is the final command that Jesus gives us before the ascension. These are our final orders from our resurrected Savior, and they are given with authority that is beyond any other authority on earth (verse 18). We are told to make disciples. Be discipled and make other disciples, my student. We are told to baptize. Be baptized, my student. We are told to teach every command. Join a church, my student, and know that God is with you always even to the end of the age (verse 20). This, buddy, is what it means to be a Christian.

What does it mean to make disciples?

_____
_____
_____
_____
_____
_____
_____
_____
_____
_____
_____
_____
_____
_____
_____